HIRING YOUR FIRST EMPLOYEE

THE ULTIMATE GUIDE FOR UK ENTREPRENEURS WHO WANT TO HIRE SMART FROM THE START

MANDY HAMERLA

Hiring Your First Employee

Legal Disclaimer

The information presented in this book represents the views of the author at the time of publication and is intended for small business owners, governed by the laws of England. It's presented for informational purposes only. While every attempt has been made to verify the information included in this book, neither the author nor any associated parties assume responsibility for any errors, inaccuracies or omissions. Case study names have been changed in some instances, to protect confidentiality.

This book aims to provide guidance that will enable you to hire a successful candidate. However, we are unable to offer a guarantee that you will hire the right person, with the right skills, at the right price, because your level of success will depend on several factors. These include your skills, knowledge, decision-making ability and role type. As these factors vary hugely from one individual to another, we cannot and do not guarantee your quality of hire.

Book design by Polgarus Studio

This book is dedicated to all ambitious entrepreneurs who want to grow their business, achieve great things and change the world.

Contents

FOREWORD

BY SHARON RAI,
ENTREPRENEUR ACCELERATION MANAGER

For an Entrepreneur, especially during the start-up phase of your journey, you'll be doing everything! And bringing in an extra pair of hands is one of the most challenging decisions you will make for your business. This is due to several factors and not least because of the fear that comes with being responsible for someone else's livelihood, or trusting someone else with your precious business.

Which brings me to Mandy and Modern HR (formally HR Refresh).

Mandy has identified these growing pains perfectly and in my view, has come up with a solution which very quickly and effectively supports any business owner with hiring their first or 100th team member. She has a wealth of knowledge built within the corporate world and has worked incredibly hard to bring solutions to Entrepreneurs that are simple to use, and cost-effective.

I have witnessed first-hand Mandy's passion for supporting Entrepreneurs and teams to get the best results for all involved. She fully understands the pressures small businesses have, as well as the emotional investment particularly for first time hirers.

Arguably your first hire should be an HR Director, to help navigate the employer landscape, focusing on building a strong, capable and motivated team and becoming a great leader. Your people are after all entrusted with your vision and potentially your biggest cost, so getting the relationship right the first time is mission critical.

So, if you want to build a healthy, productive working environment, this book will help you to build your team in the right way.

Sharon is part of the Natwest Accelerator Programme, which provides entrepreneurs with unique coaching, environments and networks required to take any business further, faster. For more details, go to:

https://www.business.natwest.com/business/business-services/entrepreneur-accelerator.html

INTRODUCTION

A few weeks ago, I got a phone call from a small business owner called Lydia.

She was in tears.

She explained that she had hired her first employee, a paid intern, to help with her social media and answer her phone and emails. However, three months after joining, the intern was still asking her lots of questions and wasn't very good on the phone, so Lydia was having to do a lot of the work herself (the stuff she was paying the intern to do).

The reason for hiring someone was to free up her time so that she could focus on her new clients, but this hadn't happened. In fact, she was even busier than before and further behind on her to-do list. She felt frustrated that she had wasted money on someone who wasn't adding any value to her business, and she wanted my advice on what she could do to fix the situation.

I asked Lydia why she'd hired an intern rather than someone experienced in managing social media. She said she assumed because the intern was young, she would know all about social media. She also said it was cheaper.

Sadly, Lydia is not alone. I've received calls from many small business owners looking for help after their new hire hasn't worked out. Sometimes, it's because the person doesn't have the right skills to do the job, but it can also be because he or she is not a great fit. Occasionally, it's because the business owner has found out that the person they hired has lied about their qualifications or employment history, which has broken the trust.

WHY PEOPLE MAKE BAD HIRES

Research by the Recruitment & Employment Confederation shows that hiring mistakes are costing UK businesses billions of pounds every year. The cost of a bad hire is approximately three times that person's base salary (i.e. someone with a salary of £42,000 can cost a business around £132,000).

The reason for this is that it's more than just the obvious costs, like the wasted job advert fees, wasted salary and wasted training costs. It's also the hidden costs you need to factor in, such as your time (both in trying to help them improve and potentially exiting them), and HR or legal fees, the duplicated time and effort of advertising for their replacement, and general confusion and disruption to everyone involved (including your clients and suppliers).

As a Virtual HR Director, working with a wide range of entrepreneurs and small business owners like you, I've seen first-hand the mistakes that people make.

Some of the most common mistakes I see are:

1. Hiring the wrong person

It's horrible when you hire someone, and it doesn't work out. This can happen when there hasn't been enough thought or planning put into the hiring process at an early stage, to identify exactly what you need or connect it to your business goals. It could also be because the selection process isn't robust enough to test their skills and values properly or no pre-employment checks have been undertaken.

In chapter 1, we'll be creating your ABSOLUTE YES criteria and identifying your DEAL-BREAKERS, so we can find someone who will be a brilliant match for YOU. This forms the basis of your entire hiring strategy and will keep you focused on hiring someone you NEED rather than someone you LIKE, i.e. it will stop your personal bias or perhaps even desperation from skewing your rational thought process and leading you to make a bad hire decision later down the line.

I'll also be sharing my top tips on how to create a robust selection process and how you can spot the blaggers, liars and exaggerators in an interview.

2. Underestimating how much it will cost

Many people focus on the salary when hiring, but it's a lot more complex than that. There are lots of extra costs to consider. The other thing that is often missed is how long it will take you to break even, i.e. cover the cost of your new hire. If you don't plan properly, you could end up with cash-flow problems, plus the added stress of someone to manage that you can't afford.

In this book, I'll cover the real cost of hiring someone, so you can go into the process with your eyes wide open and feel confident that you can afford it.

3. Not putting a robust employment contract in place

So many people don't bother with contracts, but if I could give you one piece of advice, it would be to invest in a robust employment contract. If written properly, this can help to protect you from getting screwed over, if your employee decides to set up in competition with you or work for a competitor.

In this book, I'll explain why you need an employment contract for your business and the important things you need to include, so you have peace of mind that you've done everything you can to protect yourself and your business.

WHY I DECIDED TO WRITE THIS BOOK

I know that hiring your FIRST employee can be GAME-CHANGING for your business.

Get it right, and you can achieve your goals FASTER and make MORE money.

However, if you get it wrong or make a mistake, it can drain your time and energy and leave your open to HUGE LEGAL RISKS (the kind that could destroy everything you've worked so hard to create).

But, I've discovered that many entrepreneurs don't have the skills, knowledge, confidence or support to hire someone amazing, the first time. They make costly mistakes and learn as they go – and then hire people like me to fix them.

So, I wanted to write a book that would change that.

Rather than being REACTIVE and fixing the mistakes after they've happened, I want to share with you the most important things you need to know (and do), so you PROACTIVELY hire SMART from the START. You'll learn how to protect your business and avoid making costly legal mistakes, and feel confident to deal with any issues yourself that arise.

This book is especially for UK entrepreneurs who:

- Are starting a new business and need to hire before launching
- Are at full capacity and need to hire some help to grow

- Already have a team of self-employed contractors, but feel ready to hire their first employee
- Currently, employ friends or family members, but want to expand

However, if you have already hired people, and you're looking for tried and tested strategies and tips to improve your technique and hire better quality people, you'll benefit from this book, too.

HOW THIS BOOK CAN HELP YOU SUCCEED

I'm guessing you've picked up this book because you want to hire your first employee. And you want to get it right first time.

But, perhaps you've never hired anyone before, so you're not sure on the steps you need to take; or maybe you've been burnt in the past or heard some horror stories, so you want to improve your techniques and learn how to hire from an expert.

If so, this book will help you to succeed.

It's a straight-talking, practical book, based on REAL-WORLD experience, not textbook answers.

Not only will this book take you through the whole hiring process from start to finish and teach you what you need to know (and do) to hire your first employee successfully, but

I'll also be on hand, as your Virtual HR Director, to answer any questions you have along the way.

I reveal the strategies that have enabled me to hire the best and brightest people myself, and have enabled me to help hundreds of others to do the same.

HERE IS WHAT YOU'LL LEARN

- Exactly what skills, behaviours and experience, you need to succeed
- Whether now the RIGHT time for you to hire, and if can you afford it
- The SECRET to attracting the best people to work for you
- How to interview like a PRO, plus how to spot the BLAGGERS, liars and exaggerators
- How to make a formal job offer (and what to include in your employment contract, so you can PROTECT your business)
- The boring, but very IMPORTANT things, you need to know and do as a new employer so that you can avoid costly legal mistakes
- How to get off to the BEST start with your new employee
- What to do if things go wrong and you need to fire your new employee

By the end of this book, you will feel empowered, educated and equipped to hire your first employee. Then you can repeat this tried and tested process to hire your second, third, fourth, fifth employee.

So, if you're want to avoid having sleepless nights, you NEED this book to help you hire your first employee.

Ready? Let's get started!

A PERSONAL INVITATION

Before we get started, I'd like to invite you to get in touch and let me know which role you're thinking about hiring. I may be able to offer you more customised tips to help you out, as a thank you for buying my book.

My email is: mandy@modernhr.co.uk.

Otherwise, I really hope you find this book valuable and I'm delighted that I can play a small role in your business growth journey.

Mandy

CHAPTER 1

HIRING SMART

DEFINING EXACTLY WHAT YOU NEED TO ACHIEVE YOUR GOALS FASTER

Every person you hire will either help you to achieve your goals faster or become a barrier to your success, by draining your time and energy. Which is why, this chapter is about how to hire SMART from the START, so you're set up for success from the very beginning.

We're going to focus on WHY you're hiring and WHAT exactly you need to accomplish your business goals faster. And identify who will be a brilliant match for YOU.

This forms the basis of your entire hiring strategy and will keep you focused on hiring someone you NEED rather than someone you LIKE, i.e. it will stop your personal bias or perhaps even desperation from skewing your rational thought process later down the line.

WHAT'S YOUR WHY?

When I work on a one-to-one basis with clients who want to hire an employee, one of the first things I ask is why? What exactly do you hope to achieve by employing someone and how will the appointment help you achieve your goals faster?

Knowing your 'why' enables you to identify what needs to be done and the skills required. Then the aim is to find the person who can not only do the job brilliantly but also has the right attitude and values to fit into your company's culture.

Ultimately, for any business wanting to grow, it's because you want to MAKE more money. There are four main ways you can achieve this when it comes to hiring someone.

1. To free up or better utilise YOUR time

If you're working 60+ hours a week doing everything yourself, there may be some tasks that you can delegate. This will enable you to focus on important tasks or to give you a better work-life balance, e.g. hiring a Personal Assistant to manage your diary, answer your calls and send out your invoices, or someone to pack your products and post them to your customers.

2. To be able to serve more customers by hiring someone with the SAME skills as you

If you're potentially turning customers away because you're at full capacity, then you may have decided it is time to hire someone with similar skills to you, to take on extra work, e.g. if you're a hairdresser you may need to hire more stylists to meet demand.

3. To bring in COMPLEMENTARY skills to expand your service or product range

This is when you hire someone with complementary skills to yours, to expand your current services or product offering and provide a greater customer experience, e.g. a web developer deciding to hire a graphic designer to offer logo and web design to existing customers.

4. To bring in a subject matter expert to achieve a specific outcome

This is where you identify a weakness or limitation within your skill set and decide to hire an expert to enable you to achieve greater results, e.g. a restaurant manager hiring a marketing or SEO expert.

So, the first question you've got to ask yourself is:

Why am I hiring? What exactly do I hope to achieve? It may be one of the above or a combination of things.

WHAT WILL SUCCESS LOOK LIKE FOR YOU?

Now, you've got clarity around why you want to hire; we'll spend some time defining what success looks like.

I'd like you to do an exercise that I get my clients to do when I'm helping them build their hiring strategy. Take a piece of paper and draw a line down the middle.

On the left-hand side of the line, write down all the things you want to achieve in your business over the next 12 months. Then on the right-hand side, list all the things you want to achieve personally, to improve your lifestyle.

Lucy is a Marketing Consultant, working 60 hours a week. She has two kids and a dog and desperately wants to hire another marketing professional to serve her customers and take off some of the pressure.

Here is Lucy's list:

Business Goals	**Personal Goals**
Get website revamped	Start going to the gym twice a week
Get 10 new clients	Finish early on a Friday to meet friends
Launch a new service	Change hours - start at 10am to walk dog
Run a global marketing conference	Stop working weekends - to see family

I ask people to write this list because right now, YOU are in control. YOU are choosing the hours the new hire works, where that person works and what he or she does.

The whole purpose of hiring someone is to help you achieve your goals faster. It is about making your life easier, so you're not constantly tired or rushing around or feeling resentful that you didn't go to the gym AGAIN, or aren't spending time doing what you love.

YOUR ABSOLUTE YES LIST & DEAL-BREAKERS

Now we're clear on WHY you're hiring, and the GOALS you want to achieve, it's time to figure out what you need, to achieve these things. This next section will help you refine what you need and find your perfect match.

Knowing yourself

Before we start talking about who to hire, take a minute to think about how you like to work. This is so you can understand the kinds of people you work best with (and who you can't work with) as we build up a profile of your ideal employee.

Here are some questions to use as inspiration:

- What are your strengths?
- What are your development areas?
- What do you enjoy doing?
- How do people describe your style?
- What are your values?
- What kind of environment do you work best in?
- What gets you angry or frustrated?
- What are your pet peeves?
- When are you at your best and your worst?
- Who have you clashed with in the past? Why?

Where are your skills gaps?

Based on the work we've done so far; you should now have a clearer idea of the work you need the person to be doing and how you like to work.

Essentially, it's taking your business and personal goals, then working out what you can do yourself and figuring out what the gaps are to get you from where you are today, to where you want to be.

You + them = success

If you want to free up your time, what tasks can you delegate to achieve this? Or if you want to launch a new product, are there specific skills or knowledge you need to bring in to achieve this?

The gaps will form the basis on your job description, so take a moment to think about:

- The job title – What is the most appropriate name for your job to summarise what you need? Marketing Manager, Web Developer, Admin Assistant?
- Role purpose – Why does this job exist and what work will the new employee be doing?
- Hours/working pattern – How big is this job? What days and hours do you need covering to achieve your business and personal jobs?
- What are the skills gaps you are trying to fill?
- What does the employee need to achieve (within the first six months)?
- What does success look like? You can link this back to the business goals (or projects that contribute to your business goals)

However, there will potentially be lots of people who could do your job.

So, the difference between hiring someone GOOD and someone that's GREAT is your ability to work brilliantly together. They may have the right skills, but they also need the right behaviours, attitude and values to be a great match for you and your business.

You could hire the best salesperson in the world. They have excellent sales skills to get you the results you want; but if their style is very pushy and they use dishonest tactics to get results, they may not be the right fit for you.

Creating your 'absolute yes' list

One way to achieve this by defining and prioritising the MOST important things you need to succeed. This could be the skills, behaviours, experience, traits, etc. This is to keep you on track throughout the process, so you hire the right person.

Start by writing a list of everything you want (like a wish list). Now circle or highlight the five things the person MUST have for them to thrive. These are your 'absolute yes' criteria. The person you hire must have these things. If they don't, you will automatically reject them, no matter how much you like them.

For example, if I was hiring a GP, my 'absolute yes' list could be:

- Medical degree
- DBS check (criminal record check)
- Integrity/honesty
- Excellent communication skills/articulate
- Two years' experience working as a GP in a busy surgery

There will be other desirable things, like customer service, friendly, articulate etc. but having an 'absolute yes' list keeps me focused on the things that are most important.

This list will be used throughout the selection process i.e. to shortlist your applications and ultimately deciding who to hire. Anything else they can offer is a bonus.

Identifying your deal-breakers

In addition to your 'absolute yes' list, it's also worth knowing your deal-breakers.

These are your things that should automatically lead to you rejecting the candidate, no matter how desperate you get to hire someone or how long it takes because they will drain your energy or fundamentally conflict with your beliefs or ways of working.

This is NOT about ruling out hiring anyone different from you, because it's great for you to have different but complementary strengths. Nor is it about discriminating against anyone.

This is about ensuring you don't hire someone who doesn't meet your requirements or won't perform well within your business culture.

These things are personal to you. There are no right or wrong answers, it's simply the traits or behaviours that conflict with your values or way of working.

For example, if you are a very punctual person and it is very important to be early for everything, it could be problematic to hire someone who is constantly late; or if you HATE smoking, you may find it difficult to work with a chain smoker.

Some traits will be non-negotiable. Others will not be ideal, but they are not a deal-breaker. You can learn to live with them.

Knowing yourself is key here, which is why we spent some time earlier thinking about the types of people you work best with, and the types of people you don't.

CREATING YOUR ULTIMATE JOB DESCRIPTION

This is where we connect the dots and bring everything together to define EXACTLY what you need to achieve your goals faster:

So far we've covered

- The job title
- Role Purpose

- Hours/working pattern
- The work they will be doing
- The skills you need
- Your 'ABSOLUTE YES' criteria
- Your deal-breakers

What your new employee needs to achieve within the first six months

Now we need to factor in how much you need to pay, based on what the job is worth.

How to figure out what your job is worth

The salary for your role depends on lots of factors, including your location in the UK, the industry you're in and whether you want a graduate or someone very experienced who can hit the ground running. Generally, roles have a salary band, which is the minimum and maximum you are prepared to pay, depending on the person's experience and the market rate.

There's no exact science to making sure you're paying the appropriate amount (though you need to pay at least the national minimum wage), but there are a few easy ways to help you get it just right.

1. Look at online job boards

There are countless online job boards, so choose the ones you like the feel of or the ones you know people in your industry use when they're looking for a new role. Approach it as if you're the one looking for a job and fill in the search function with the criteria of the role in question. You'll end up with lots of great information about what other companies are paying for similar roles. There may be a big difference in salaries for the same role, and this will also depend on the industry, experience of the individual, level of complexity of the job, level of responsibility and location.

2. Call local recruitment agencies

Many recruitment agencies are happy to tell you what the right salary should be for a role. Give your local agency a ring and ask the responsibilities and what you are looking for, and they will give you an idea of the salary.

3. Search for online salary benchmarking services or reports

There are websites devoted to providing salary data. They do a lot of the hard work for you! Some examples are Michael Page, Glass Door, Salary Search and PayScale. They all differ. Some provide salary information reports for free, but you might have to pay if you want more of a detailed report.

4. Ask people in your network

Ask your contacts working in a similar field to see if anyone is willing to share salary information with you.

NEXT STEPS

I hope by now you have a job description that is directly aligned to help you achieve your goals faster, and you feel much clearer about what you need and why.

Let's move on to assess whether you are ready to hire your first employee and look at:

- Is now the right time?
- If it is, can you afford it?
- Should you hire an employee, or would you perhaps be better off hiring a worker or a freelance contractor?

CHAPTER 2

ARE YOU READY?

IS NOW THE RIGHT TIME AND CAN YOU AFFORD IT?

There's no doubt that deciding to hire your first employee can be difficult for many people.

If you hire too early, you could have cash-flow problems or an employee without any meaningful work to do, and the added stress of someone to manage.

Alternatively, if you hire too late, you could lose valuable clients, miss out on an amazing opportunity because someone else gets there first or start losing clients or receiving bad reviews because you can't cope with the volume of work.

This chapter aims to validate that:

1. Now is the right time for you to hire

2. You've factored in all the costs, and you can afford it

3. You need an employee, rather than a worker or a freelance

contractor which could be other alternatives to get the outcome you want.

IS NOW THE RIGHT TIME?

There's no exact formula to decide when it is the right time to hire, but here are some common reasons some of my clients gave, when they knew it was time to hire their first employee.

1. The quality of work is consistently suffering

For David, it was due to his poor quality of work: "I knew I had to hire someone when I was constantly apologising for missing the deadline. The quality of my work was consistently getting worse because I was rushing from one job to the next. It bugged me that people would think badly of me, as I do care about doing a great job."

2. You're working yourself to the bone

Helen said she decided to hire her first employee because she was working herself to the bone, and it wasn't sustainable, nor enjoyable. She got to the point where she was working every weekend just to keep up, which wasn't sustainable. She knew she was headed for burn out if she didn't make a change.

3. You're surviving, not thriving and want more success faster

Amanda had big ambitions but felt like she was on a hamster wheel and couldn't get off. She was exhausted trying to do all the work herself to grow her business. She believed in her business model and wanted to take a risk and invest in someone to get results faster.

4. You're mentally ready to delegate

John said he hired a Virtual Assistant (VA) previously, but it wasn't successful, because he didn't delegate work to her. He said that even though the VA was very good, he struggled to let go. However, over time, he realised the only way to free up his time was to delegate.

5. You're starting to hate your business

Verity loved being creative, but she felt a lot of her time was spent doing non-creative things, such as logistics and operations. She started to lose passion for her business to the point where she was becoming unproductive. She knew she needed someone to take over the operations and admin if she wanted her business to work.

Do any of these reasons resonate with you? Go back to your 'why' and think about whether now is the right time. Now, let's move on to how much it costs and whether you can afford it.

HOW MUCH WILL IT COST?

Many people get caught in the trap of thinking the salary is the only cost to factor in. However, the cost of a new employee goes way beyond the person's annual salary.

Before you hire, it's important to be aware of (and include) all the hidden costs, so you know how much hiring someone will cost you and therefore whether you can afford it.

Calculating the total cost of a new hire

Depending on your situation, here are some additional costs you may need to factor in:

Recruitment costs: These start at around £199. On a job board like Indeed, you can set a maximum daily rate, and they will let you know roughly how many applications you can expect for the price. However, going through a recruitment agency can cost approximately 15% of the base salary.

Salary: In chapter one, we covered how to decide on the potential salary you'll need to pay. You need to be able to pay this on the same date each month, no matter how much money you make, to avoid breaching the terms of the employment contract.

Pension: Because the UK government has an auto-enrolment scheme, you need to factor in any pension costs that you are required to pay. The only way to avoid this is if the person you hire opts out, but you won't know this until you hire them. The rates are going up each year

Benefits/perks/expenses: There is a whole range of other benefits you could introduce, including health insurance, dental insurance, enhanced sick pay, paying for them to get a qualification, Perkbox, extra pension, life insurance, etc. Even if you don't want to offer any of these, if your employee will be doing a lot of travelling or you take them out for a monthly lunch/coffee then it all adds up, so you need to factor in this cost.

Payroll fees: You may need to pay your accountant to process your payroll if you prefer not to do it yourself.

Tax and National Insurance: You will need to include the amount that you are required to pay for tax and National Insurance.

Premises: If you currently work from home, will you need to rent somewhere for the two of you? If so, make sure you factor in this cost.

Equipment: You might need to purchase a laptop, software, a mobile phone and other tools to accommodate a new hire if you don't have them already. Even the cost of shared file storage needs considering.

Insurance: Once you become an employer, you need to have employer's liability and public liability insurance, so you need to factor that in.

Training: If you want to keep employees, you need to invest in their development on a regular basis. You can hire people to run the training or you can provide training yourself, so put a price on what that will cost you for your time.

Other Considerations

Here are a few other things to consider in your costs

Will you pay less if your contractor will become an employee?

Contractors generally earn more than someone who is an employee with the same job, because they have less security and the likes of holiday, sick pay and training are not part of the remuneration.

If you're converting a contractor that works for you to an employee, it's worth looking at your new total cost. If you need to break-even by reducing their hourly rate, have an open conversation with the contractor to explain why and how you have calculated it.

Will you be offering any incentives?

Incentives are linked to performance and can encourage the

individual to stay loyal to the company. They are generally an investment to incentivise results and the right behaviours. You may not want to offer this from day one, but it's worth knowing the options available to plan for any future costs.

Bonus scheme – A bonus can be a great way to incentivise staff as you can build it to reward and celebrate great results, based on individual achievements, the company's success or both. This works well if the individual has a big project to achieve or has specific targets to hit. Some bonus schemes will only pay out if the company hits certain financial targets, so you have the security that you will only pay out if you can afford it.

Commission – Commission is an arrangement in which you pay your employees a percentage of sales they bring to your company. Often companies will pay a lower base salary if they offer commission, but this will depend on the nature and demands of the job. This works well with sales or business development roles.

Profit-share schemes – This is where you share the profit you make with your employee. It generally works by setting a target of how much profit you forecast you'll make. Should you make a higher profit than the target, a portion of this extra cash will be shared among your employees. This can either be paid as a set amount to all employees or as a percentage of salary. However, popularity for profit-share schemes has dwindled since tax breaks were phased out by the government in December 2002, to make way for share incentive plans. They work best where profit is the main key performance indicator.

Or, will you offer share plans?

Share plans are popular with tech start-ups that want to attract great people but can't offer much job stability or cash up front. This is where you give away company shares to your employees.

Many start-ups offer an Enterprise Management Incentive (EMI) share options because they are tax-advantaged schemes that can be highly beneficial for both the company and the individual option holders. Please be aware that EMI options aren't available to all, and you will need to check that both your business and the proposed option holders meet certain criteria for HMRC to approve the scheme.

Take a minute to tally up all the potential costs you will incur based on hiring this person, so you have a better idea of how much it will cost you. Now let's look at whether you can afford to hire an employee.

CAN YOU AFFORD IT?

Now you have a good idea of how much it will cost; let's look at whether you can afford it.

The most important thing to consider is cash-flow, i.e. how much money comes in vs how much is going out. Hiring someone is a long-term win, so in the short term, you might not get much return on your investment until they have settled in. So, having enough cash to cover the first six months is incredibly important.

Forecasting

To do this, you can forecast what impact hiring someone will have on your business. It's often worth looking at planning for best, most likely and worst-case scenarios, so, for example, if you hire a consultant, and you don't get new clients straight away, you have enough cash to ensure you can afford to pay their salary for around six months after joining while they get out and build relationships

You can do this by:

1. Estimating your future sales

Based on your past sales and additional resource, work out how much revenue you expect to bring in. Think about what's realistic for a new hire to generate in the first month or year. How many extra products could you produce or how many more customers can you serve? If they are freeing up your time, how much more can you do? Just remember that in most cases, it will take a time for employees to reach their full money-generating potential. That's why it is critical to confirm that you can cover the cost of a new hire even if that person doesn't immediately contribute to the bottom line. While anything can happen – and you could come in under or over – your estimated projections will tell if you can swing a new hire or if you should wait until things pick up.

2. Working out the additional costs

How much will this cost you in both upfront and ongoing costs? Are you able to cover the unexpected, such as a laptop breaking? Are there any big expenses coming up that could deplete your cash-flow and cause issues?

3. What's the overall impact on your profit margin?

For every pound you spend, how much profit do you expect to make? If you estimate that you will still turn a profit, or it should be beneficial in the long-run, then you should feel confident that you're ready to hire.

How it's looking? Do you feel ready to hire an employee? If not, I'll also cover a few other alternatives for you to consider.

OTHER ALTERNATIVES

If you have a more seasonal business or you can't afford to hire a full-time employee right now, you do have other hiring options. You can hire a self-employed contractor, worker, temporary or part-time employee to come in and alleviate some of the burdens. You can spend as much as you can afford, and still get some needed support. Which leads me to explain the difference between them.

Employees vs. Contractors

There's often a lot of confusion around employees, workers and self-employed freelances or contractors, so I thought it would be useful to begin by clarifying what the differences are and why it matters. Then you can decide which is best for you, right now.

Regarding the law, an individual doing paid work in the UK falls in one of three main categories.

- An employee
- Self-employed contractor/freelance
- A worker (which has a very specific legal meaning)

This is called the employment status.

Here are the main differences

1. Employees

Employees are great if you want stability, continuity and more control over when and how the person works.

Employees will carry out the work personally that you need them to do. They have rights, such as holiday allowance, to be paid minimum wage, receive sick pay and receive a payslip and generally will work to the terms within a contract of employment. Full-time and part-time employees are essentially the same. The difference is what it says on the tin – a full-time employee works longer hours.

You can also hire an employee on a fixed-term contract, which is for a specific period (such as to cover absence or maternity leave) or until a set task has been completed. This is good if you want to have a trial period with an employee, to begin with, before fully committing.

2. Self-employed contractors

Contractors are great if you want an injection of expertise in a very flexible way, without the commitment

Freelance, consultants and contractors may be employed by another company or be self-employed. They decide where and when they work and who does the work, provided they deliver the requirements of the brief. They generally look after their taxes and National Insurance contributions and do not have the same rights as employees. They typically work for lots of companies.

3. Workers

Workers are great if you have a seasonal business, where

demand fluctuates, and you need a flexible workforce. Zero-hours contracts fall under the worker category.

Workers are kind of in between an employee and a contractor. They have no set hours and are just paid for the hours they complete. However, they will accrue holiday pay and are entitled to the minimum wage. You don't have to give them work, and they have the right to refuse work.

The table on the next page explains the key differences

Criteria	Employee	Worker	Contractor
How are they paid?	PAYE (your payroll)	Usually PAYE	They invoice you
Are they entitled to company benefits?	Yes	Some	No
Can they decline work?	No	Yes	Yes - or they can assign work to other people
Do they use company equipment	Yes	yes	No - generally use own equipment
How long will they work for you?	Indefinite amount of time	Occasional work to cover seasonal peaks	Usually for a project/fixed period
Who sets the hours of work?	You do	You both do - could be a zero hours arrangement	Contractor sets the hours, based on your brief
Who has control over how the work is done?	You do	You do	They deliver in line with the brief
Do they attend your team meetings?	Yes	Some	Rarely
Can they work for other people?	No usually	Yes	Yes
What type of contract is required?	Employment contract	Casual worker/zero-hours contract	Terms of engagement

What about hiring interns?

Interns are usually undergraduates or students. Most internships last for any length of time between one week and 12 months. Generally, they are still learning their craft, so will need nurturing and guidance.

The word 'intern' doesn't exist in law, so a paid intern will generally be an employee or a worker and should be paid the national minimum wage.

However, internships can be unpaid where they are for less than one year as part of a UK-based further or higher education course, they are school work placements (i.e. under 16, working for a week or two), they are volunteering for a charity or they are work shadowing, i.e. observing someone else and not carrying out work.

Interns can be great if you want some general support, or you manage to find someone incredibly talented at a much lower cost.

Why it matters?

Getting the employment status right is very important. It's not just about what's written on paper. It's also about how you treat the person in practice. If you start blurring the lines and treating a contractor as an employee, you could find yourself in trouble.

Let's look at a real-life story, which you may have read about in the press.

Uber, the taxi company, hired its drivers as self-employed contractors but allegedly treated them like workers.

In 2016, two of their drivers took Uber to an employment tribunal. They argued that they should be classified as 'workers' not self-employed contractors because of Uber's control over their working conditions. Uber denied this.

However, the drivers won the case, and the court said they should be entitled to worker conditions, which included the national minimum wage, holiday entitlement, parental leave and more, potentially backdated for the last six years. The case is still ongoing, but Uber may potentially end up having to pay this to all their drivers (which could be up to around 40,000 people).

A situation like this could potentially bankrupt a business. Which is why it's important to get the employment status right.

NEXT STEPS

Based on everything you've learnt so far, do you feel ready to hire your first employee?

There are pros and cons to hiring an employee, over a freelance contractor or worker. Ultimately, it depends on what YOU need.

If you're not sure, you can always trial this by hiring a freelance contractor or an employee on a fixed term contract, e.g. for three months, to test your assumptions before you commit to hiring someone on a permanent contract.

If so, let's move on to the next chapter to start attracting the best people to come and work for you.

CHAPTER 3

ATTRACTING THE BEST PEOPLE

INCLUDING HOW TO BUILD A DESIRABLE BENEFITS PACKAGE ON A BUDGET

Have you ever visited a popular job site, such as Indeed or Reed? They are PACKED full of jobs. In fact, Indeed claims that 9.8 new jobs are added each second globally.

If you were looking for a new job, it's unlikely you'd have the time or the will to look at all the jobs that could be right for you. Depending on how in-demand the role is, it could just be a small handful.

This is why having a brilliant HIRING STRATEGY is essential.

In this chapter, we will be focusing on how you ATTRACT the best people to work for you, by doing three things.

1. Building your ideal employee AVATAR (so you know what they want).

2. Identifying the right places to post your job advert, (so your employee avatar sees your job advert).

3. Using this insight to create a job advert that will stand out in a crowded market and convince your employee avatar to apply for your job.

YOUR IDEAL EMPLOYEE AVATAR

One of the easiest ways to attract the best people is to build what's called an employee avatar. This is often done with customers, and it's the same process, but just about who you want to work for you rather than who you want to serve.

You can do this by asking yourself:

- What's their background?
- What's most important to them, regarding their career?
- Where will they look for jobs?
- What benefits would they find most attractive?
- What's the kind of environment they will thrive in?

This exercise is designed to get you into the mind of the person you want to work for you and figure out what you can offer and what aspects of working for you that you can highlight to get them to WANT to work for you.

In turn, this will help you decide where to advertise and what to include in your job advert to convince the right person to apply for your job.

Find out what they want

Different people want different things – such as money, working with nice people, having a purpose in life – and this can change, depending on the stage you're at in your life.

It's not a one-size-fits-all approach, and you need to think about what's going to be most attractive to your ideal employee.

The best way to find out what they want is to ASK people who would fit the criteria.

Mike owns a café, and he needs to hire a part-time waitress. The café is very close to a school and would be perfect for a local mum. Mike decided it would be nice to offer free food as his main benefit and thought he could perhaps pay a bit extra into the pension scheme because that was important to him.

However, before advertising his job, Mike did some research to find out what was important to local mums. They told him school hours, holiday entitlement and money were most important. So, when he decided to advertise his job, he highlighted school hours and a generous holiday package, plus he made a point of saying the person appointed would keep all tips. He realised that a pension scheme wasn't a priority for his employee avatar.

Give them what they want

Once you know what your employee avatar wants, you can seek to create a desirable benefits package for them, which can be achieved on a zero or shoe-string budget.

Here's a list of some popular benefits for you to get you thinking.

Extra holiday

The minimum holiday you can offer is 20 days plus eight bank holidays. But this is a benefit that isn't an extra cost and one that's in high demand. Or you could give them their birthday off or time off over Christmas if you close the office.

Childcare vouchers

This is a great benefit because it shouldn't cost you anything as an employer, with the tax and National Insurance savings, but the individual can save around £1,000 on the cost of childcare.

Gym membership

With many gyms now costing less than £20 a month for off-peak, this is a great low-cost benefit to offer.

Flexible hours

Could you allow someone to start earlier or later to enable them to have a better quality of life? Or perhaps work from home once or twice a week?

Staff discounts

If you can offer discounts on your services and products, this is an easy win. You can also ask around in your local area, as many companies are happy to give discounts to other businesses within the community.

Food

Offering food is a great benefit. This could range from having breakfast together once a week, which you pay for via expenses, to providing drinks and snacks by stocking up from somewhere like Costco.

Other things

There is a whole range of other benefits you could introduce – including health insurance, dental insurance, enhanced sick pay, paying for them to get a qualification, Perkbox, extra pension, life insurance– but ensure you choose benefits that will be attractive to your ideal employee.

WHERE TO ADVERTISE YOUR JOB

The whole purpose of advertising a job is for the right people to see it and want it i.e. VISIBILITY.

There are hundreds of places that you can choose to advertise your job, but the aim is to get it in front of the right person, i.e. your employee avatar.

So, you need to think about where YOUR employee avatar will be looking for a job and advertise your job there.

Here are some ideas to help inspire you:

- Your network or networking events – You may be able to get a referral from within your network. Or ask them to share your post or spread the word through their network
- Your social media channels – If you have a big social media following, advertise on your channels. If someone is already following you and passionate about what you do, this is ideal. You could create a video or graphics to make it more visually appealing

- People on your email list – If your customers could be potential employees, this is a great way to target people
- Popular online job boards – Here are a few to look at
  Indeed – https://www.indeed.co.uk
  Reed – https://www.reed.co.uk
  Simply Hired – https://www.simplyhired.co.uk
- Industry-specific job boards or magazines, e.g. artsjobs, retailchoice, charityjobs etc.
- Start-up online job boards such as:
  www.workinstartups.com
  www.ukstartupjobs.com
  www.techstartupjobs.com
- Local newspapers – they often have jobs sections for specific types of roles
- Local noticeboards – your local supermarket, post-office or library may be great for you
- Local Facebook groups – for example, a local mum groups, if you are looking to target working mums.
- University and college job boards – great for interns or work placements
- Flyers through doors in your area – Great for jobs like hairdressers, cleaners and retail roles
- Little cards with your orders saying you're hiring

- Competitions where you ask people to tag potential candidates, in return for prizes

If you're short on time, you could ask a local recruitment agency to manage this for you.

What the professionals do

If you want to be super savvy, you can do what the professional recruiters do and leverage the power of LinkedIn to target people who aren't looking for a job but could be tempted to move for the right opportunity.

If you have a good network, you can do this yourself, and you can start by performing straightforward keyword searches. Just go to 'Advanced people search' and type in key search words and parameters to find people with those keywords on their profiles. The more specific you are, the narrower the search.

You can then look at 'People also viewed'. This is another function of LinkedIn that recruiters use as it shows people with similar roles and skill sets as often these will be similar people and of interest to your search.

You can also join industry and skills-based LinkedIn Groups, and carefully follow their discussions and take an active part in their postings. This allows you to observe who the experts are and who is contributing to conversations in a meaningful way.

Then you can make a list of the people you want to target and aim to connect with them and message them directly to see if they are interested in your opportunity.

You could always take advantage of the free upgrades LinkedIn offers, which will give you a greater ability to search for a specific period to be able to target people outside your network.

WINNING JOB ADVERTS

Most job adverts are boring. They are simply 'wish lists' of lots of things the company wants.

So, you need to create a job advert that stands out in a crowded market, not one that people will look at and then move on to the next one.

However, you also want it to RESONATE with your ideal employee. You want people to look at it and think *'that sounds like a great opportunity and the kind of place I would love to work'*, and then decide to apply for your job.

Finally, once people decide they want to apply for your job, you need to make it easy for them: no applications forms that take hours to complete. Equally, though, you want to STOP any time-wasters from applying

So, essentially creating a compelling job advert, that is visible to your ideal employee avatar, is the secret to your success.

How to convince people to apply for your job

Now you know what your employee avatar wants and what you can offer, you can use this insight to create a job advert that will stand out in a crowded market, make sure the right people see it and convince your employee avatar to apply for your job.

Here are a few tips to help you create a winning job advert

1. Show your personality – Make your advert creative, fun and interesting.

Most adverts are just boring job descriptions. The same two-page wish list of things that do nothing to make people think, *Wow! That job sounds good.*

Think about how you can make it more fun and interesting, by showing your personality and challenging the status quo. This could be funny, witty text or even a picture or video.

Here's a great example of an advert that stands out from the norm and will make you smile.

2. Explain the two-way exchange – what do you need and what's in it for them?

Include the reasons you set out earlier regarding why someone should want to work for you.

What else can you offer them? Is it a fun place to work, will they be able to be creative or have work autonomy? Will they have task variety, flexible hours or work-life balance? Can they work from home? Are you a kind boss? Ensure you include the things that your employee avatar will find attractive in your advert.

Also, incorporate your 'absolute yes' list into the advert to make it clear what you're looking for, to avoid being inundated with applications from people who are not suitable for the role.

3. Make it different (and interesting)

Whether it's capital letters, colours, choice of words or it just looks different; you need your job advert needs to stand out.

For example, setting a challenge can bring out the competitive side in people. It could be something like: *We are looking for the best Marketing Assistant in Birmingham. Is that you?* Or perhaps a mathematical challenge for a data scientist or a problem to help solve.

People are curious by nature, and having a job advert that is a bit intriguing can convince people who wouldn't normally be interested in applying.

4. Include killer questions

Some job sites allow you to add killer or knock-out questions.

These can stop time-wasters from applying for your job.

For example, if I was hiring an HR Manager, my killer questions could be

- Are you Level 5 CIPD qualified?
- Have you managed a team of 3+ people yourself?
- Do you have a valid UK driving licence?

If applicants say no to any of these questions, the job site automatically rejects them.

You can link these killer questions to your 'absolute yes' and deal-breaker lists.

What to do if you're not attracting the best people

You can generally advertise your role for as long as necessary, to ensure you have some great people to choose from. The general rule is to start with two weeks, so you can see who has applied.

But, if you find your advert isn't attracting the right calibre or the number of people after two weeks look at what you can do differently. Can you advertise it in more places, or can you improve the wording? You can always ask people for feedback to ensure it's received well by your target audience.

NEXT STEPS

Now you've got a great job advert which is going to bring great people to apply for your job. In the next chapter, we'll focus on how you can interview like a pro to ensure you choose the best person.

CHAPTER 4

HOW TO INTERVIEW LIKE A PRO

INTERVIEWING TECHNIQUES, PLUS HOW TO SPOT THE BLAGGERS, LIARS AND EXAGGERATORS

Once you've advertised your job, and you've got some great people that have applied to work for you, you can arrange to interview the best candidates.

An interview is your opportunity to find out more about them, to see who will be the best fit for you and ultimately help you to achieve your goals faster.

If you've never interviewed before or you think you're interviewing skills could be better, this chapter is for you. By the end of this chapter, you'll know:

1. How to look and sound professional during interviews

2. How to choose the right interview questions to ask

3. How to gather evidence (and spot the blaggers, liars and exaggerators)

Ultimately, you'll know how to interview like a pro so that you can make the RIGHT decision.

HOW TO LOOK AND SOUND PROFESSIONAL

Have you (or anyone you know) ever applied for a job, gone to the interview and come home afterwards feeling like it had been a complete waste of time?

If so, perhaps it was because of:

- The interviewer being late – meaning you are not their top priority
- The interviewer doing most of the talking – so you feel like you haven't had the opportunity to showcase what you can do
- The interviewer being distracted by his or her watch/phone/other people – signifying boredom or lack of interest
- The interviewer asking random questions or was not adequately prepared
- The interviewer being unprofessional or asking inappropriate questions

If you want this hire to work out, you need to ensure the people who apply have a great experience, by thinking about what impression you want to give, how to best represent your brand and how to ensure at the end of the interview, they want to work for you.

How to impress your candidates

Apart from the obvious, like show up on time and be courteous and polite, here are three things you can do to look and sound professional.

1. Create the right environment

When the candidates turn up to the interview, you want to impress them immediately and create the right environment that mirrors what you're all about.

If you currently work from home it might not feel appropriate, or safe even, to invite strangers into your home, so you may need to arrange somewhere to hold them. Here are some suggestions for you to consider.

- Need somewhere informal? An obvious one is a local café. Those based on the quieter back roads might be a good bet, rather than the usual high street coffee chains. Scope it out in advance. There's nothing worse than finding it's really popular and too cramped and noisy. See if you can even book a table or, if not, make sure you get there early to secure the best table.

- Need somewhere private? If you're planning on discussing anything confidential or sensitive, find a location where you and your interviewee can talk freely. Your local library or community space might have meeting rooms for hire.
- Want to convey a cool vibe? Check out whether there are any remote working hubs or co-working venues in your area that offer meeting spaces. Or try any local trendy boutique hotels. Often, these places will have very stylish and comfortable interiors and allow you to book meeting rooms.
- Don't need to meet in person? Video conferencing technology like Zoom or Skype can be great. It's practical, cheap and easy to use, but you might miss out on some of the usual social interactions you take for granted by meeting face to face.
- Need to present a professional image? If you have a good relationship with a local professional services business, like a law or accountancy firm, they might lend you a meeting room at their offices if you're a valued client.

2. Make a great first impression

Wear an outfit that makes you feel confident and looks professional.

Offer your interviewees a firm handshake and begin with some small talk before the interview.

3. Perfect your selling pitch?

Can you explain your vision, what your company does and why this is a great opportunity in less than five minutes?

Interviewing is a two-way process. So, you also need to convince them why they should work for you.

ASKING THE RIGHT QUESTIONS

Many interviewers waste theirs and their candidate's time asking poorly thought-out questions. Some even Google a list of generic questions and ask those.

To increase your chances of hiring the right person, it's worth investing time to plan your questions for each candidate you interview. Think carefully about the knowledge, skills, expertise and character traits you need for the role, and develop your questions around these. Also, make sure you ask questions to see if the candidates would thrive in your working environment and team. Cultural fit is just as important as the skills they have.

Deciding which questions to ask

You only have a limited about of time for each interview, so you need to choose your questions wisely. At the end of the interview, you want to feel confident (and get as much proof as possible) that the person you want:

1. Has the skills to do the job brilliantly

2. Has the right personality and values to thrive in your company's culture – i.e. you can work brilliantly together as a team

3. Has the flexibility or potential to take on more in the future, as you seek to achieve your vision

Ultimately, every question you ask should have a clear purpose and should connect to your 'absolute yes' list and your deal-breakers – to gather evidence for you to decide whether they are the right person for you or not.

You can ask any question you like, as long as it's helpful. A good way to start is by listing out all the questions to test what's on your 'absolute yes' list and will help you get to know the candidates. Then pick questions that will test your deal-breakers.

Interviewing techniques

Once you know what you are going to cover, there are different techniques you can use to phrase how you ask the questions to maximise the value you can get from the answer. Here are some of the different ways you can ask questions:

Open-ended questions

In a well-conducted interview, the candidate should be talking for up to 80% of the time. One way you can ensure this is to pose questions that are broad and open-ended. As well as getting the candidate to talk, this approach will also help reveal some of his or her attitudes and priorities about the topics discussed:

'Tell me about…'

'Could you give me your impressions of…?'

'What experience have you had of…?'

'Give me an example…'

Previous experience

There is a considerable correlation between performance in the past and predictions of success in the future. It is, therefore, useful to gain an understanding of exactly what the candidate has done in the past and to what depth. Make sure you read their CV, and if there's anything of specific interest that aligns what the role you have, focus on that:

'Tell me about the change project you led at Company X and what results you achieved.'

Behavioural

Ask the candidate to describe specific past situations where they may have used the behaviour you are trying to assess:

'Tell me about a particular instance when you had to work under pressure to achieve an important deadline.'

'How have you dealt with an irate customer who isn't happy about the service they have received?'

Hypothetical

This is when you ask a hypothetical question to see how they would deal with a certain problem or situation:

'How would you handle a customer that tried to bribe you to get a free product?'

Probing

Candidates frequently give responses that seem incomplete or appear to be 'textbook answers'. You should draw out further information from the candidate until you are satisfied the questions have been answered.

'Could you expand on that?'

'What was your particular involvement with that?'

The way you ask the question will steer the answer you get, so it's worth thinking about how you can extract the information you need to make an informed decision.

AVOIDING THE WRONG QUESTIONS

I've sat in many interviews where I've been left cringing, where a business owner has asked an inappropriate question that could get them into a lot of trouble.

I've heard business owners ask candidates about their kid's ages and schooling because they wanted reassurance that the person would be able to come to work on time. On another occasion, the interviewer asked the candidate's age because they wanted to understand how long the person planned to work until they retired.

These questions were not meant to cause upset or offence, but they could have been perceived as discriminatory if the person didn't get the job. And they felt this was because of their role as a primary carer (mum) or their age.

How to stay out of trouble

There are some questions which are off limits because they could be perceived as discriminative (people can still sue you for discrimination even if they don't work for you). But, even if they don't sue you, it's important that make people feel welcome and comfortable.

So, here are the 10 questions you shouldn't ask a candidate during a job interview, from a legal perspective.

1. How old are you?

This is now irrelevant as there is no fixed retirement age. Asking this could lead to an age discrimination claim. Also, it's just rude to ask someone their age. If you're worried the person is too young, you could simply ask if they are over 18.

2. How much longer do you plan to work before you retire?

Again, as above, this is no longer necessary. Because people can work to whatever age they choose.

3. How many days' sick leave did you take in the last year?

This is often asked to test reliability, but someone could feel it's discriminatory because of their illness or disability. Instead, you could ask: How many unscheduled days of work did you miss last year. You need to remove the element of sickness.

4. Do you suffer from any type of disability?

This is often asked with good intentions to see if there's anything that the company needs to do to support them, but it's not appropriate to ask during an interview. You could ask this after you have made a job offer to check whether any reasonable adjustments are required.

5. Do you have childcare arrangements in place if we need you to work outside of your normal hours?

The word 'childcare' here is the problem. Instead, you could ask something like: *Are you available to work overtime on occasions? Are you happy to travel to visit our clients at short notice?*

6. Do you have any criminal convictions?

Unless you are FCA regulated (in finance) or working with children or vulnerable adults, and therefore need the person to undertake a DBS check, it's against the law to refuse to employ someone because of spent convictions in some roles, so you shouldn't ask.

7. Are you from the UK?

This isn't relevant to the role so shouldn't be asked. You can ask: *"Are you eligible to work in the UK?"*

8. Is English your first language?

Again, this is not relevant to the role, so shouldn't be asked.

9. How far would your commute be?

This sounds like a perfectly reasonable question, but could get you into trouble if the person thinks you're not hiring them because you think the commute could be too much for them (age) or because of their parental responsibilities. Instead ask something like: "**Are you able to commit to starting work on time, at 9am?**"

10. What's your religion? Will you need time off because of it?

Again, this is inappropriate. Instead, you could ask: Are you happy to work the days/hours as set out in the job description?

There are many other questions, you shouldn't ask, so when you plan the questions you want to ask just think how they could be perceived by someone? Is there anything that could accidentally get you into trouble?

Bushra Noah v Sarah Desrosiers

One of the most interesting legal cases I remember from when I was studying employment law, was about a Muslim lady called Bushra Noah, who sued a small business owner called Sarah Desrosiers because she didn't get the job she applied for.

Sarah owned a hairdresser salon in central London, that specialised in 'urban, funky, punky' cuts and was looking to hire an additional hairdresser.

Bushra applied for the job and was invited in for a trial. At the end of the trial, didn't get the job. She claimed it was because of her headscarf, as the staff were required to have their hair visible, as part of the salon's image and she wasn't able to.

She decided to sue the hairdressers for religious discrimination and claimed she was owed £34,000 in compensation, after being turned down for a job because of her religion and for lost earnings.

Sarah faced a three-day employment tribunal and endured four hours of cross-examination. She said

> 'I managed to defend myself and not cry, but it was incredibly difficult,' she says. 'I'd even had to ask my accountant, who is a Muslim, and another Muslim friend to write letters confirming that I am not racist. The whole experience was so humiliating and, most importantly, unnecessary.'
>
> 'I kept thinking: "I've worked hard all my life – how can it be possible that someone can come into my shop, talk to me for ten minutes and then sue me for £34,000? How is that possibly fair?'

The case went to court and the tribunal ruled that while Bushra's claim of direct discrimination failed because there was no evidence that she wasn't hired because of her religion, her claim for indirect discrimination succeeded because ultimately the reason she didn't get the job was because of her headscarf, which is part of her religion.

Sarah was therefore ordered to pay £4,000 compensation by way of 'injury to feelings' i.e. for the upset it caused.

You can read Sarah's full story here: https://www.dailymail.co.uk/femail/article-1027300/How-I-nearly-lost-business-refusing-hire-Muslim-hair-stylist-wouldnt-hair.html

SPOTTING BLAGGERS, LIARS AND EXAGGERATORS

Even if you ask the right questions, in the right way, one of the biggest challenges is that candidates can misrepresent themselves, which can lead to a bad hire. How can you tell if a job candidate is lying during an interview?

Trembling hands. Sweaty. Red face. No eye contact.

Do you think these are traits of someone lying or just someone very nervous under the stress of being judged and getting a job? It could be either.

So, unless you're a psychologist or detective, it's worth taking a more robust approach when it comes to sussing someone out if you feel worried.

This is not about tricking people or tripping anyone up. It is purely about taking proactive steps to ensure that you make the right decision.

Here's how you can do it:

1. Create an atmosphere that encourages honesty

If you can encourage them to be honest with you, without fear of repercussions, they will be more inclined to be truthful when it comes to the reason for leaving their last company.

2. Introduce hiring tests to complement your interview

For example, if you want to hire a hairdresser, watch them cut hair. If you want to hire a waitress, ask them to wait on tables for 15 minutes. If you want to hire a dog walker, take them out with you to see how they cope. Or if you want to hire a coder, give them a whiteboard and a problem to solve. You are looking for EVIDENCE to prove they have the skills they claim to have.

3. Ask the same question twice

If they tell the story differently or contradict themselves, call it out and see how they react.

4. Watch out for them being too vague in their answers

You can use the probing interviewing technique to draw out the information you need. This is asking more questions to get them to expand on their answer and see if they struggle with the details. If they do, it's probably a made-up answer.

5. Ask to see proof

For example, if they claim to have a degree or professional qualification in something, ask them to bring their certificates to the interview.

6. Analyse their CV

When looking through a candidate's CV, check the dates add up, or check if there is a considerable unexplained gap. Or maybe some vital pieces of educational details are missing, such as A-Levels, or their final degree grade.

7. Get references from their former employer

If they said they worked as a Marketing Manager for five years, ask their former employer. Sometimes people say this, but in reality, they've worked in a much more junior role.

8. Take notes or use a scorecard

Use your 'absolute yes' list as a school card that allows you to score each person to see how comes out best on paper. Never used one before? I've explained how to create one below.

9. Watch out for 'we'

Sometimes people tell you a story, but they focus on' we'. If so, ask them to focus on their specific contribution, and what they did, to avoid them taking credit for someone else's achievements.

10. Get a second opinion

You can ask a friend to interview with you to see who they think is the most genuine and who you would work best with.

How to create your interview scorecard

An interview scorecard is a document that helps you keep track of the conversation and keeps you focused. It can also help you to ensure consistency and fairness and protects you from employment claims of discrimination because you can show how you came to your hiring decision.

An interview scorecard should include three things:

1. The attributes being scored, i.e. your 'absolute yes' list

You'll need to think about how you measure these. Some will be easy, e.g. having a specific qualification, but others are harder to quantify. Provided you are fair and consistent; it will do the job.

2. Assigned weighting to each attribute, where appropriate

Some things on your 'absolute yes' list will be more important than others, so placing a weighting on the most important things will ensure you focus on what's most important. To weight an attribute, you can use a 1–5 scale.

3. Checks to spot deal-breakers

If you stumble across any deal-breakers, you will know this is not the right person, and you can reject them on this basis.

Then at the end of the interview, you calculate the score for each individual and then the premise is that you would hire the person with the highest score.

If you have a gut feeling someone is great or not great, try and support this with evidence to avoid hiring someone or ruling someone out without a good reason.

As I've mentioned in previous chapters, it's important to ensure you hire the right person by preparing thoroughly, asking the right questions and getting evidence to ensure the person meets the requirements for your 'absolute yes' list and does not possess any of your deal-breakers.

As you interview each person, a good way to keep you focused is by having a framework that enables you to score each person you interview.

NEXT STEPS

So, now you've met everyone and decided who you like, you can start the process to make a formal job offer.

CHAPTER 5

MAKING A JOB OFFER

WHAT TO INCLUDE IN YOUR EMPLOYMENT CONTRACT AND EMPLOYEE HANDBOOK TO PROTECT YOUR BUSINESS

Congratulations!

You've found someone amazing to hire and now it's time to make them a job offer.

In this section, we'll focus on:

1. What to say if they try and negotiate or ask you for MORE money

2. The documents to prepare that make up a formal job offer

3. How an employment contract and employee handbook can protect your business and reduce your risk

Your first step

Once you've decided who to hire, your first step is to call them to give them the good news. Most people will think about your offer, although some will accept straight-away.

It's always best to discuss their salary expectations early on, and share how much you are paying at the interview (or earlier), to avoid wasting time. However, sometimes, even if you've done this, candidates may still ask if you can pay more and will try to negotiate the salary, so let's talk a bit more about how you can prepare for this.

SALARY NEGOTIATION

Now, I've known some business owners to get angry when someone tries to change the goal posts and negotiate the salary. It can sour the job offer, take the excitement away from it and replaces it with stress and delay.

Try not to look at it this way. It's part of the game, and it's worth having a plan in place, so you know how to respond if you're put in this situation – and having a bit in reserve. You don't want to pay a higher salary than you can afford.

If you do get asked for more money, here are your options:

1. Is there something else you can offer instead of a salary increase

Perhaps a small bonus if they hit certain targets after six or 12 months? This ensures you give more money after you have seen some results – and it's a one-off payment, rather than an ongoing commitment.

2. Setting the salary at 10% less than you can afford from the start

So, you have a bit in your back pocket to play with if you need it.

3. Say no

Of course, you can explain that this the salary and there is no flexibility to offer anything more at this point, but remind them of the other benefits you are offering. If you had two great candidates to choose from, this is a viable option, as you don't have to start the process all over again if they turn down your offer. However, don't reject any of the other candidates until you have a definite yes – as you won't want to eat humble pie by going back to them and making them feel like second best.

It's important you remain assertive and in control throughout the negotiation process.

If they are vague about what they want, you should put the onus on them to tell you what they are expecting to avoid a ping-pong negotiation.

If you do counteroffer, it's worth stating that this is your final offer, to avoid them coming back with another request.

THE FORMAL PAPERWORK

Once they've accepted your job offer, it's time to send out the paperwork to formalise the arrangement; but what exactly do you need to send and why?

Here's a list of things you should be sending:

- Offer letter – a friendly letter to give an overview of what's included in the job offer pack and the deadline for returning the paperwork
- A contract of employment – to set out the terms and conditions on offer and protect your business
- Personal details form – to collect relevant information to be able to set them up via payroll and notify HMRC
- Reference nominee form – so you can get contact details of their former employers to request a reference, and get their permission to do so

- Employee handbook – this is a document that contains all your HR policies, so they know what is expected of them and practical information such as how to book a holiday or what to do if they are off sick
- Employee handbook acceptance form – a document to confirm they have read the employee handbook and agreed to comply with the policies. This is evidence if they break a rule and claim they didn't understand or weren't aware of it
- Privacy policy acceptance form – this is a GDPR requirement
- DBS Check Information – if relevant
- FCA additional checks – for companies that are FCA accredited

If you don't have time to prepare these documents yourself, you can buy template packs via my website.

https://www.modernhr.co.uk/employmentscontracts

A contract of employment is an agreement between an employer and employee and is the basis of the employment relationship. Most employment contracts do not need to be in writing to be legally valid, but it is better if they are. A contract 'starts' as soon as an offer of employment is accepted.

You may think that employment contracts or HR policies are unnecessary, or be tempted to find a free template on the internet, but a well-written contract and employee handbook (which consists of your HR policies) can protect you and your business from being fined, sued or screwed over, and avoid misunderstandings that could lead to conflict or disputes.

What should be included in an employment contract?

There are some important factual clauses to include, which are mostly common sense: these are things like the date employment started (or is to start), pay, job title, place of work, notice period, etc.

However, there are some additional, more sophisticated, clauses that often get left out of basic employment contracts – especially if you buy an off-the-shelf, cheap one, from a non-HR or legal expert.

Here are the clauses you should be including:

1. Probation period

If you hire a new starter, but it's not working out (e.g. the person doesn't have the skills they claimed to have an interview), it is possible to terminate their employment if you have a probationary period (like a trial period) built into their contract. I would always recommend having a probation period of around six months and having a notice period of one week during this time.

2. Restrictive covenants

These are specific restrictions placed on employees when they work for you, but also for a set period after they stop working for you, up to around 12 months. They include non-compete agreements and protect you from things such as your employees working for a competitor, setting up in competition with you, poaching clients or staff, etc. They protect you from making a loss as a result of actions taken by your employee (or former employee).

3. Confidentiality

This is to ensure they will not disclose any confidential information to anyone, either during or at any time after they have left the company, which could cause a loss to the company or have a detrimental impact on the reputation of the company.

4. Pay in lieu of notice

This means you can pay them a lump sum for their notice period. This is useful if you want them to leave immediately.

5. Garden leave

This is where you can stop them from working during their notice period if you don't want them to be on site or in touch with your customers.

6. Outside employment

This restricts them from taking on any other jobs while they work for you.

7. Intellectual property

Without an intellectual property clause, you may find that you do not own the rights created by your employee, or worse, that your employee is entitled to future payments.

8. Contingencies

These are like caveats of the job offer. They could be things such as satisfactory references, providing their highest academic certificate or qualification, having the right to work in the UK or passing a DBS check.

The most important HR policies to have?

There are lots of different policies to choose from, but I would suggest you have the following policies as a minimum, to comply with your legal obligations as an employer:

- Absence
- Capability
- Disciplinary
- Grievance
- IT Security
- Equality
- Flexible Working
- Performance management
- Holiday and leave
- Health and safety
- Parental
- Privacy (data protection)

How detailed they and how much emphasis you place on them depends on your business type. For example, if you are FCA regulated, you may have a more heavyweight policy around anti-bribery; but if you have a manufacturing business, the priority should be a more robust health and safety policy.

Some companies have very formal policies for everything; others have just a few that are written more informally. There's no right or wrong, and policies should be written in line with your employer brand, the tone of voice and industry, relevant and help you to ensure the smooth running of your business.

NEXT STEPS

Once you have created all the job offer documents, you can send this out to your successful candidate, with a deadline of when you need the paperwork returned.

CHAPTER 6

THE BORING (BUT IMPORTANT) BIT

THE THINGS YOU NEED TO KNOW (AND DO) AS A NEW EMPLOYER TO AVOID COSTLY LEGAL MISTAKES

Now you're going to be an employer; there are a few practical things you need to know (and do) that this chapter will make clear:

We'll cover:

1. The five things to do TODAY, as a new employer

2. What employees are entitled to by law

3. The three most common reasons why employees sue their employer (just so you know)

5 THINGS YOU NEED TO DO

As someone that's probably very busy running your business, it can be tempting to skip some things or allow them to fall to the bottom of your to-do list.

So, here are the five things I recommend you do, as a new employer:

1. Get insurance

Every UK business that employs one member of staff or more is required by law to have Employer's Liability Insurance. This insurance covers your business if an employee is injured at work or who becomes ill (because of their work), and claims compensation. Often Public Liability Insurance is also required.

It's important to note that Employer's Liability Insurance is only valid in the United Kingdom. This means that if your company has employees based outside the UK, you will need to check the employment laws in those countries and take out any necessary policies.

You must be able to show it to the Health & Safety Executive upon demand (or you could face a fine of up to £1,000).

Other types of insurance you may need include motor insurance (if you operate any sort of vehicles), professional indemnity (e.g. for lawyers and accountants) and public liability, which covers the cost of compensation for personal injuries and loss of or damage to property.

2. Get references from their former employer

If you haven't already done this, it's worth requesting a reference from their former employers at this point. You will have the contact information you need to do this from the job offer paperwork you gave them and this also means they have permitted you to do so (this is important to get). If you do it before they have even resigned, it can be very awkward.

The general rule is to take up two references from previous line-managers. If they haven't worked for their former companies for long, then you can ask for more references. If you are FCA regulated or work in an industry that has specific requirements, you should consider asking for references covering the last five years of employment. You can call/email or write to them to ask them for a reference. There are no strict rules.

Regarding what to ask, keep the questions relevant, appropriate and focused on the person's abilities and aptitude and not too long-winded. However, with GDPR, you will need to inform the individual upfront of the information you want, via your privacy policy and they will also have access to it, if they ask.

When you receive the references, match up the detail with the CV. For example, check the start and leave dates and job title are the same as it stated on the person's CV. If there are any concerns, then give them a ring.

3. Check they have the right to work in the UK

Every company is accountable for checking the person they hire is legally allowed to work in the UK. The government has a very strict process on this you are required to follow. If you have not carried out the correct checks, you could face a penalty of up to £20,000 for each illegal worker, and if you employ someone who you know (or have reasonable cause to believe) is an illegal worker, you can face an unlimited fine and up to five years in prison.

In a nutshell, you are expected to comply with the law and prevent illegal working in the UK by carrying out 'Right to Work' checks on people before employing them, to ensure they are lawfully allowed to work. The 'Right to Work' checks means checking official documents to ensure the individual who will be joining your company has permission to work in the UK. You should ideally ask your employee to bring in proof of their right to work in the UK before they start working for you, but if this is not possible, it must be on their first day of employment.

At present, people from many countries within the European Economic Area automatically have the right to work in the UK, such as France, Germany and Poland. The current list of EEA nationals who may work without restriction can be found here: https://www.gov.uk/eu-eea.

However, we are yet to see what implications Brexit has on this.

To check the right to work, there are three key steps you need to take:

i. Obtain – You need to ask for a copy of their ID that proves their right to work in the UK. There is a specific list of documents the government will accept as proof that talks about List A and List B, which refers to the type of documents needed to provide to prove the right to work in the UK. List A is where people have the permanent right to work in the UK and List B is where people have a temporary right to work.

See: https://www.gov.uk/government/publications/right-to-work-checklist

ii. Check – You should check the documents carefully to make sure they are valid (e.g. it is their name and picture, and it's in date) and prove the individual has the right to work in the UK. Some people will have a permanent right (i.e. British people and people from certain countries in Europe). Others will have a limited right to work (such as a limited number of hours per week, or for a certain period or a specific project/company), so you need to make a note of this and conduct further checks in the future. Further details about the checking process are provided below to help you with this.

iii. Photocopy – Take a photocopy of the main page with their picture in front of the individual and then write on the photocopy 'Certified to be a true copy of the original. This Right to Work check was made on [DATE] by [NAME]' and add your signature. Keep the copy in a safe place, ideally their personnel file.

Even if the person has a British accent or tells you they were born in the UK; you still need to follow the Right to Work checks. This applies to everyone that you employ.

4. Set up payroll

This is often outsourced to an accountant, but if you decide to run payroll yourself, you need to complete certain tasks to pay your employees for the first time. You can choose when and how often to pay your employees.

For full details go to:

https://www.gov.uk/browse/employing-people/payroll

Below is a summary of the key steps you need to take.

- Register as an employer with HM Revenue and Customs (HMRC) at: https://www.gov.uk/register-employer

- Get a login for PAYE Online:
  https://www.gov.uk/paye-online:
- Choose your payroll software to record employee's details, calculate pay and deductions, and report to HMRC. There are lots of free options, such as BrightPay and Capium, as well as paid options, such as SAGE.
  https://www.gov.uk/payroll-software
- Collect the data you need: full name, bank details, National Insurance number.
- Tell HMRC about your employees:
  https://www.gov.uk/new-employee
- Record pay, make deductions and report to HMRC on or before the first payday.
  https://www.gov.uk/running-payroll
- Pay HMRC the tax and National Insurance you owe each month.
  https://www.gov.uk/running-payroll/paying-hmrc
- Complete reports as required. You'll also need to complete certain annual reports and tasks to prepare for the next tax year, which starts on 6 April.
  https://www.gov.uk/payroll-annual-reporting

5. Create a safe place to store the employees' data

It's important that you store the documents in a safe place and password protect any documents that contain personal data, e.g. address, date of birth etc. Generally, you should set up personnel files, one for each person you hire.

YOUR LEGAL OBLIGATIONS

Employers have a duty of care to their employees, which means that they should take all steps which are reasonably possible to ensure their health, safety and wellbeing.

Demonstrating concern for the physical and mental health of your workers shouldn't just be seen as a legal duty – there's a clear business case, too. It can be a key factor in building trust and reinforcing your commitment to your employees and can help improve staff retention, boost productivity and pave the way for greater employee engagement.

As the law is constantly changing, you can read more about your legal obligations here: https://www.gov.uk/employing-staff.

But I've listed below some important things you need to be aware of:

National minimum wage – There is a minimum amount that each person must be paid per hour. There are different amounts, depending on age, and this increases each year.

Pension – It is now compulsory for all businesses, regardless of size, to offer a pension to their employees. This is called auto-enrolment because everyone eligible will go into the pension scheme unless they choose to opt out. You can find out more about what to do via the Pensions Regulator website – www.thepensionsregulator.gov.uk

Holiday entitlement – All employees, including casual staff, are entitled to 28 days' holiday each year, (if they work full time). This includes eight days of public/bank holidays. You can use the handy calculator to work out someone entitlement if they start part way through the year

https://www.gov.uk/calculate-your-holiday-entitlement

Protection under health and safety law – The employer must ensure, 'so far as is reasonably practicable' the health, safety and welfare of workers, – which includes minimising the risk of suffering stress at work.

Access to a grievance procedure at work – Grievance procedures are used for considering problems or concerns that employees wish to raise with their employers.

Statutory redundancy pay – Employees you make redundant might be entitled to redundancy pay – this is called a 'statutory redundancy payment'.

Maternity/paternity/adoption/parental leave – This sets out the entitlements that parents have by law

Many of these can be covered simply by having all the essential HR policies in place that are accessible to your employees.

HOW TO AVOID BEING SUED

Guess how many people sue their employers each year?

The most recent figures (up to 31st March 2020) show that 103,984 cases were accepted by the employment tribunal service over a 12-month period. Many more people tried to make a claim, but for a multitude of reasons their claims were rejected. This could be because they weren't eligible (you need to have two years' service to claim for unfair dismissal) or they were too late (you have set deadlines to prevent people going back years and years after the event happened).

When employees make a claim, they generally do so for more than one reason, for example, discrimination and unfair dismissal. This is advised by solicitors, because they may win in one area but not another, and, because of the complexity of the law, it's good to cover all basis and try for as many as they can.

How much would it cost?

At the time of writing this guide, the highest sum awarded in a tribunal was £1,762,130, which was for a sex discrimination claim. This is when you are treated differently (badly) because of your gender. This kind of fine can bankrupt even the most financially stable company.

Now, before you start panicking, I want to assure you that in my experience most people don't want to sue you. They do it because they feel they've been treated badly: and when I say badly treated, this could be anything from them feeling bullied through to them feeling unfairly treated.

However, what's important here is how THEY feel. He or she may not have been badly treated in your opinion, but when people feel their core values or morals or sense of fairness have been compromised, they may do or say things that are out of character. If it's not nipped in the bud, it can end in an employment tribunal.

The three main reasons why your employee could sue you

Here are the most common reasons why your employee could sue you (and how to prevent it):

1. Unfair Dismissal

In its simplest form, unfair dismissal is when your employment contract is terminated, and your employer did not have a fair reason to do so. It can also be claimed if you did have a good reason to fire the individual, but you didn't follow the right procedure, i.e. the disciplinary process, correctly.

The highest award for an unfair dismissal claim was £470,865, which will have involved an unfair dismissal claim where the statutory cap did not apply. The average award for unfair dismissal was £13,851.

Tips to prevent unfair dismissal claims:

If you need to dismiss someone, always follow the disciplinary procedure, known as the ACAS Code. This involves an investigation and a formal invitation to a meeting and hearing (like a mini court case, but within our company). Even in circumstances where it's a no-brainer – for example, you catch them stealing from you, or you witness them discriminate against someone – you must follow the process. Without doing so, you leave yourself wide open to an unfair dismissal claim, and you can be penalised for not following the process.

2. Discrimination

Discrimination can take many forms. Generally, it occurs when an employee or job applicant is treated unfairly because of their race, gender/gender reassignment, nationality, religion or beliefs, age, sexual orientation, status or class, disability, or familial status (pregnancy, specifically).

It's possible to discriminate against someone even if you don't intend to. For example, you can discriminate by offering working conditions or rules that disadvantage one group of people more than another.

If you're a business owner, you're responsible for any form of discrimination carried out by your employees, so it's important that you can prove you've done everything you can to prevent or stop it.

There's no cap on how much someone can win for discrimination claims. As mentioned previously, the highest sum currently awarded in a UK tribunal was £1,762,130.

Tips on how you can prevent discrimination claims:

- Introduce an equality policy
- Tell your team you take a zero-tolerance approach to discrimination
- Have an anti-bullying policy and grievance policy, and tackle complaints quickly
- Be observant to what's happening within the team and potential issues

3. Breach of Contract

An employment contract is a legally binding document.

A breach of contract is where the terms in the employment contract are broken, e.g. you change someone's job or reduce their salary without consent.

If the employee can prove they have lost out financially because of a breach of the contract, they may be able to claim compensation. The maximum award that the tribunal can make for breach of contract is £25,000.

Tips to avoid a breach of contract:

Ensure you understand the wording in the employment

contract you give out. It's if too much legal jargon or a template off the internet you found, you won't understand what you're signing up to. Then you can ensure that you don't breach them.

For example, if your contract says you must pay a bonus every year or give a pay rise every June, you'll need to do that, or you could be breaching the terms of the contract.

NEXT STEPS

The reason for including this paragraph is simply to help you understand how you can avoid making costly legal mistakes by accident.

Hopefully this has given you a deeper understanding of how to stay on the right side of the law.

CHAPTER 7

GETTING SET UP FOR SUCCESS

PLUS, WHAT TO DO IF THINGS GO WRONG AND YOU NEED TO FIRE HIM OR HER

By now, everything is in place, and you're just waiting for your new employee to join your business.

Your final challenge is to get your new employee to be productive as quickly as possible and build loyalty – so you don't lose them.

However, this isn't always easy.

Perhaps the 'control freak' side of you may struggle to delegate effectively and end up micro-managing them. Or maybe, you struggle to bond, because you can't spare the time to get to know them properly.

So, I wanted to include details in this chapter to help you get off to the best start, and ensure all your hard work hiring this brilliant person pays off

By the end of this chapter, you'll know:

1. How you can get the best out of your employee

2. How to delegate (without losing control)

3. What to do if it's not working out

Why bother?

Here are the three biggest risks in not planning for your new employee starting:

1. They become disengaged, quickly

Imagine how disappointed you'd be if you were excited to start your new job, and upon arrival, it feels like your boss wasn't expecting you. If you don't create a warm and welcoming environment, all that initial enthusiasm the employee feels around joining you gets lost, and it's hard to turn this around.

2. They won't know what they're supposed to be doing

If you don't get clear from the outset with your new employee on the purpose of their role, where they fit into your business and what your expectations are for success, you risk assumptions being made around work priorities and areas of focus.

3. They decide to leave

The worst-case outcome is that your new employee resigns within a few months after joining because they are unhappy, they're not clear on what their focus is, and they don't feel like they fit in. This is a bad outcome for all involved and means you have to go through the whole time-consuming and costly recruitment process again.

GETTING THE BEST OUT OF YOUR NEW EMPLOYEE

When you've been used to working in a team of one, you have been doing things your way, but when you become a team of two, you need to think and act differently.

You need to manage, motivate and communicate with the other person.

Five steps to success

If you want them to be as productive as possible, here's how you can to set them up for success:

Provide direction and clarity – Explain to them your vision, your goals and what you are trying to achieve so that they can help you. It's no good keeping things back from them if you need them to help you.

Give them the information they need to do their job – This could be access to files, context, history and client insights. Who do they need to meet with or be introduced to?

Offer the right tools and equipment – Let them hit the ground running, by ensuring you have ordered all the tools and equipment they need. For example, if they need a laptop or business cards, have this ready from day one. Otherwise, you're going to lose valuable time when they could be out selling.

Give them permission to be proactive – Finally, new employees tend to wait for instruction. They don't want to do the wrong thing, so, give them permission to be proactive, rather than them sitting and waiting for the next instruction.

Get to know each of them – One of the most powerful things you can do is to get to know your new employee, which is about figuring out the best way to work together and getting a deeper understanding of what will motivate your new employee. Let me explain a bit more about how you can do this.

Getting to know each other

My clients use my 'getting to know each other' exercise, to help with this.

The way it works is that both you and your employee have a piece of paper (as shown below with an example) which you complete separately. Make sure you spend time thinking about this to get it right.

Then you come together and share your list and talk through how you can get the best out of each other.

My strengths	**My weaknesses**	**Please do**	**Please don't**	**How I communicate best**
I work brilliantly under pressure. I love public speaking and working with clients	Financial analysis	Give me praise and thank me when I've done a good job	Embarrass or blame me in front of customers	Daily 10 mins to ask you questions

This is a great tool to have an open and honest conversation. You will learn so much about each other and agree on things like how often to meet and how not to press each other's buttons. You'll also know where they can add the most value and the areas they are not so strong.

As the manager, you can set out your expectations and boundaries in a way that's informal but impactful.

You can also swap bits of paper and pin them to your notice boards as a reminder.

How you can use this exercise in different scenarios

This exercise can be used by everyone, no matter who you've hired. Here are some examples of why you'll find it beneficial.

Your contractor becomes an employee – Unless you've been treating your contractor like an employee, the dynamics should change when your contractor comes an employee. The biggest change is that you'll have more control over how they work, so you should look at giving them more training and feedback, so they continue to develop and grow. The other change is that they will need to start asking permission for things they perhaps didn't have to ask before – like to book a holiday or letting you know if they are off sick. So it's worth sitting down with them and using this tool to discuss how them becoming an employee changes how you work together and nipping in the bud any annoying habits or things they do that you want to change.

You've hired a friend – Hiring a friend (or friend of a friend) can be great because you know you get on personally. But, working together can be completely different, and it can be tricky when it comes to the difficult stuff, like you have to turn down holiday, them not performing properly, etc. It's worth using this tool to discuss how you will work together and what you expect of each other to ensure you are both on the same page.

You've hired a stranger – Over the first few months, you'll be getting to know each other, learning each other's styles and how to work best together. As the manager, it's worth you driving the conversations around what you expect and explaining what they can expect from you, like you telling them where you'll be, what to share with them, etc.

Research shows that people leave managers, not companies. Don't let that manager be you.

HOW TO DELEGATE, WITHOUT LOSING CONTROL

It's true that delegation can feel difficult and uncomfortable, but it doesn't mean you need to lose control.

What you need is a way to delegate the right things, but also know it's been completed. The 'Getting to know each other' exercise we did earlier is great for this. Your 'please do' could be 'please do drop me a quick email to confirm when you've completed a task' or 'please do copy me to emails you send to our VIP clients' (so you know what's been said).

How to decide what you can delegate

In principle, you'll be looking to delegate the things you identified as part of the job description. However, in case things have moved on or changed, you can focus on your to-do list, and generally, put things into three buckets:

Do it yourself – These are the most important things that only you can do. You may be inclined to put everything in this bucket, so make a conscious effort to be strict with yourself. Otherwise, this becomes a pointless exercise.

Delegate it – These are tasks that need doing but don't rely on you doing them. They are better suited to your new employee. Taking the time to communicate what needs doing and by when is key, to avoid frustration, confusion and misunderstandings.

Ditch it – These are things on your to-do list, but they are not essential, maybe even no longer relevant. These tasks can come off your list.

Then you ask them to focus on the things you can delegate.

If you're worried about losing control, you can track everything you've delegated and asked them for a daily or weekly update when you first start working together, so you have peace of mind that things are getting done.

Be mindful, though, that you are still trying to build a relationship and micromanaging them should be avoided wherever possible.

As part of the 'getting to know me' exercise you can explain that you've not delegated before, so they realise it's not personal. If they're very good, they may proactively ask you for work or tell you what's been completed.

WHAT IF IT ALL GOES HORRIBLY WRONG?

If your new joiner has started working for you, and it's all going wrong, it can be stressful, upsetting and generally very deflating.

You're probably wondering what happened to that amazing person you interviewed, who promised you the world but isn't cutting the mustard.

But, although it's disappointing, I want to assure you that if you do hire someone that's not right, it's not the end of the world and it is fixable.

The good news for you is that employees have fewer rights if they have less than two years' service – so if you fire them, they can't claim for unfair dismissal, which is a big one. However, they can claim for discrimination and other things, so it's still important to be fair and reasonable and to document what you are doing and why you are doing it, to minimise risks.

Earlier I talked about the importance of having a robust employment contract. And when something like this happens, it's easy to see why.

So, make sure you have these three things in place to make life easier:

1. A probation period

Having a probation period (trial period) for all your new hires, of around three to six months is essential. If you feel like it's not working out, you can terminate the person in a relatively straightforward way. To minimise risk, you should give them feedback and the opportunity to improve (over a few weeks); but if it's still not working, you can follow the disciplinary process to fire them.

2. Ensure you have a shorter notice period during the probation period

Have a shorter notice period during the probation period is also useful. One week's notice during probation is common.

Otherwise, you're stuck with them working for you for a longer period, which can be awkward and you will have to pay them for the duration of the notice period.

3. Include a capability and disciplinary policy in your staff handbook

Have a clear policy and procedure for managing poor procedure is helpful. It could be covered as part of your disciplinary policy or as a separate capability procedure. Make sure your procedures, in writing and practice, follow the ACAS Code of Practice.

The practical steps you need to take

You should follow your disciplinary process to minimise. This doesn't mean it becomes a long and drawn out for new employees, but it should be fair, reasonable and documented.

1. Try to improve performance informally first.

As part of your regular one-to-one meetings, discuss your concerns informally with the person. Be absolutely clear on the gap in their performance, e.g., what they are or aren't doing, and what it is they need to do to meet your expectations. Be as specific as you can and give them actual examples, so they understand the issues. Ask open questions and find out if there is anything holding them back and anything you can do to support or help them. Give them the chance to improve and show that they can meet your expectations. A lot of performance issues can be turned around informally, but not always.

2. Follow a formal process to dismiss the employee

If you've tried to deal with this informally, but you haven't seen enough of an improvement in the person's performance, and you don't believe the situation can be turned around, this is when you need to follow a formal process.

Even though there is no risk of unfair dismissal, it's a good idea to consider the whole picture and weigh up any other risks: for example, has the employee made any complaints, had an accident at work or taken a lot of time off sick? Also, do any of your policies or employee contract clauses refer to how you handle poor performance? If they do, make sure you follow your process.

Let the person know you're going to be having a formal meeting to discuss their performance. Set out in writing very clearly the details of the meeting and specifically what the performance or capability issues are. Give the person a reasonable amount of time to prepare for the meeting and give them the right to bring along a work colleague or a trade union representative.

Present the information and examples to the person and explain your concerns and the impact on the business. Ask them to comment and give them the chance to explain their side. Take notes of the meeting, or better still, arrange to have a neutral person to take notes.

If nothing else has come to light that changes the situation and you're clear that giving the situation more time to improve is not going to help, then write to the person without delay after the meeting to confirm the outcome to end their employment. Give them the right to appeal the decision. If they want to appeal, wherever possible, arrange for someone else who hasn't been involved to hear the appeal process.

3. Learn from it

Reflect on what went wrong – and how you can prevent this from happening again.

Ending someone's contract is never easy, regardless of the reasons and causes, but if you follow the process in this book, the aim will be for you to avoid being in this situation.

NEXT STEPS

So, we have now covered the whole hiring process, from start to finish. Let's move on to your next steps and how I can answer any questions you may have.

CHAPTER 8

YOUR NEXT STEPS

WE'VE COVERED A LOT IN THIS BOOK, AND I HOPE YOU FEEL MORE EDUCATED, EMPOWERED AND EQUIPPED TO HIRE YOUR FIRST EMPLOYEE.

You should know:

- EXACTLY what and who you need to achieve your goals faster
- How much it will cost and whether you can AFFORD it
- Where to advertise your job to attract the BEST people to apply
- How to look and sound professional (and feel in control) during the interview
- How to ask the RIGHT interview questions and spot blaggers, liars and exaggerators
- How to make a formal job offer – and what to say if they negotiate and ask for MORE money (than you can afford to pay)

- How to prepare all the important documents, including how to create an employment contract that protects your business
- The steps you need to take to meet your legal obligations (and the common reasons why your employee could sue you)
- How to get the best out of your new employee

So, now it's time for you to start the hiring process and find someone amazing that will help you achieve your goals faster.

Got questions?

In case you have any questions about anything I've covered, or want support through the hiring process, then email me at mandy@modernhr.co.uk.

Could I ask a favour?

If you've found this book useful, I'd be very grateful if you could provide me with a review.

Best of luck – I'm here if you need anything. Do email me if you have any questions on mandy@modernhr.co.uk

Mandy

ABOUT THE AUTHOR

MANDY HAMERLA

Mandy Hamerla is a Virtual HR Director for Tech-Startups, Creatives & Charities with less than 300 people and the founder of www.modernhr.co.uk - a popular resource for UK entrepreneurs and business owners.

Mandy helps entrepreneurs and small business owners to grow and scale their business, by building an amazing team and avoid costly legal mistakes.

She has helped hundreds of people to hire the best and brightest people and managed and led large global teams herself, so she knows first-hand the challenges and benefits that come when you can build a great team.

She has a Masters Degree in HR & Employment Law and is a Fellow of the CIPD qualified (the highest qualification in HR).

KIND WORDS ABOUT MANDY

Jessica Rose, London Business School

"Mandy is a dream to work with. We worked together at a very difficult time in my business when I needed some support with staffing and managing challenging situations; Mandy made the process clear, calm and professional, she is incredibly skilled at what she does.

If you are looking for help with ANYTHING to do with HR, staffing or hiring someone, I would 100% recommend Mandy. It made such an impact on my business to have her as a professional guiding me through a process to find a resolution.

It can be hard running a business on your own and having HR support on your side is not always the first investment you think of but working with Mandy is worth every penny".

Gautam Pandey, CopoFi Ltd

Mandy has been a perfect HR partner for our company. Not only has her service been able to take all HR related matters off our very busy plate but helped and guided us in the very important employee strategy. Her service helped us with all our hiring documents, policies and process.

Additionally, she was able to review and advice on all our employee decision and being meticulous throughout. Her experience enables her to provide enterprise-level service for a startup environment.

A great find and thanks again for everything and we look forward to continuing to work with you.

Tom Marren, Coventry Scales Ltd

Like many small companies, we didn't fully appreciate HR. Whilst we knew we needed the basics as an employer, we always viewed additional HR services as something that would be costly for our business. However, spending just a few hours with Mandy at Modern HR completely opened my eyes to why HR is just as important in a small business, and how it doesn't have to cost the earth.

From the outset, it was clear Mandy had done her research on our company, and she had the knowledge and experience to advise what we needed to do to make sure we had the right policies in place. Mandy provided us with a policy package specifically tailored for our business which will support our employees and us as we grow.

I would absolutely recommend Mandy; she certainly made my experience hassle-free, easy and affordable.

ACKNOWLEDGMENTS

I'D LIKE TO OFFER A HUGE THANK-YOU TO:

My Dad for all his advice, support and guidance on publishing my first book

My husband Brent and my sons Luca & Jake for giving me space and time to write

My Mum & Sisters for their encouragement

Mike Sweet for suggesting I write this book

Janet Murray for her support and inspiration

Sharon Rai for her coaching and belief in me

And all my wonderful clients and entrepreneurial friends and everyone else who took the time to help me

GLOSSARY

Applicants – People who apply for your job.

Behavioural Interviews – Employment interview where the candidate is asked to give specific examples of past behaviours that show how he or she behaved in certain situations.

Candidate – Individual who has completed all assessment requirements for a specific position and is eligible to be considered for the certified pool.

Cash-flow – Money that comes in and goes out of a company. It is the generation of income and the payment of expenses. Cash inflows result from either the generation of revenue through the selling of goods and services, money borrowed, or money earned through investments.

Competencies – Measurable or observable combination of knowledge, skills, abilities, and other related behaviours necessary to successfully perform a specific job.

Employee – Someone who works for you who will carry out the work personally. They have rights, such as holiday allowance, to be paid minimum wage, receive sick pay and receive a payslip.

Employment Status – Defines the rights and responsibilities that an employee has at work, and therefore determines what is required from the employer.

Freelances/contractors – Freelancer or contractors may be employed by another company or be self-employed. They will therefore often look after their taxes and National Insurance contributions and have no rights, unlike an employee. They typically work for other people, and you need to be careful not to treat them like an employee.

Job Advert – This is a brief description of the job role and is the first thing a candidate will see when choosing a job to apply for. This is where the department needs to describe the key elements of the job and make it engaging. It also holds key information surrounding the contract type, salary, interview, closing date and job title.

Job Analysis – A structured and defined process of gathering, analysing and synthesising information about a job to identify and describe the duties, tasks, knowledge, skills, abilities and other detailed characteristics necessary to perform the job.

Job Description – A general statement of job duties and responsibilities.

Skills – A present observable competence to perform a learned psychomotor skill of physical job performance.

Sourcing – Exhaustive searching and networking methods used by recruiters to find (source) and attract top talent to vacant positions.

Zero-hours Worker – A zero-hours worker is in between an employee and a contractor. They have no set hours and are only paid for the hours they complete, but they will accrue holiday pay and are entitled to minimum wage. You don't have to give them work, and they have the right to refuse work.

Printed in Great Britain
by Amazon

62715285R00078